Hey there!

I'm super psyched to **GUIDE** you through this **JOURNAL**, but first, there is an important issue at hand ... **WHO ARE YOU?** Let's start documenting this shit!

What is your name?

How old are you?

What is today's date?

~~Please enclose a lock of your hair here~~

Just kidding! Don't do that. Ever. That's so fucking creepy!

Now all I need is your signature and we're basically bonded for life! (kind of)

X _____

So, how have you been lately?

WHAT'S
POPPIN'?

self portrait

DRAW WHO YOU USED TO BE. FOR BETTER OR WORSE.

WRITE DOWN THE FIRST MEMORY THAT COMES TO MIND FOR EACH YEAR OF YOUR LIFE UP TO THIS POINT

(it's okay if you don't really remember the first few years. you were a baby! give yourself a break!)

0:

1:

2:

3:

4:

5:

6:

7:

8:

9:

10:

11:

12:

13:

14:

15:

16:

17:

18:

19:

20:

21:

22:

23:

24:

25:

26:

27:

28:

29:

If you are 30+ and using this journal, you can stop right now. I imagine you already know everything there is to know about yourself and the world. Congrats! I mean, that is the way it feels when you turn 30... right? RIGHT? Oh, fuck. Okay, in that case, keep going with this exercise and the rest of this journal!

drawing of meaningful place from your past

CHILDHOOD
BEDROOM
EDITION

drawing of meaningful place from your past

CLASSROOM
EDITION

drawing of meaningful place from your past

THEIR PLACE

— you know who!

LIVE ~~WITHOUT~~ REGRET!

(regret is the spice of life, right? right, guys?!)

TOP 3 MISTAKES I'VE MADE:

1:

2:

3:

write a letter to a younger version of yourself — at a time when you needed a lot of love

Yo! Ya wanna feel awesome/terrible?

CREATE A HOOK-UP CHART WITH YOURSELF AT THE CENTER SURROUNDED BY YOUR FORMER, UM, "LOVERS"? YEAH, LET'S JUST SAY LOVERS. THEN EXPAND IT TO INCLUDE WHO THEY'VE HOOKED UP WITH. AT LEAST THE ONES YOU KNOW ABOUT. CONTINUE INTO INFINITY.

THIS IS A GREAT WAY TO ANALYZE CONTEMPORARY DATING & MATING WHILE REMINDING YOURSELF TO <u>DEFINITELY</u> USE <u>A CONDOM</u>!

Pull a Craig David and "Fill Me In"
(Does anyone get that reference?
Anyone? Hello? Is this thing on?)

People I used to look up to

Literary
Mag

Listen, we've all created highly embarassing things in our past that seemed really truthful & good at the time. Step into your younger self, embrace the awful, and write the most cringe-worthy poem about your past.

VENT TO ME

An Apology

for actions from my youth

yesyesyesyesyes

yesnomaybeyesnomaybe

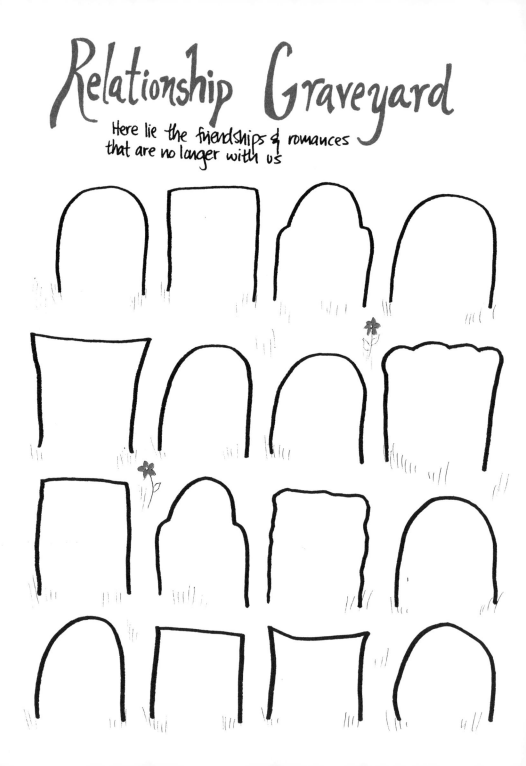

DISH TO ME

self portrait

DRAW WHO YOU ARE | RIGHT NOW. IT DOESN'T HAVE TO BE A LITERAL INTERPRETATION. OR IT COULD BE. DO NOT OVERTHINK IT. UNLESS YOU HAVE A STRONG DESIRE TO OVERTHINK IT. OKAY, NOW WE'RE JUST WASTING PRECIOUS TIME. GO FOR IT!

What's cookin', good lookin'?

SOUNDTRACK TO YOUR LIFE

1. THE "I'M BORED AT WORK" SONG:

2. THE "WAITING FOR SOMEONE TO TEXT BACK" SONG:

3. THE SONG THAT REMINDS ME OF COLLEGE:

4. THE "LOOKING THOUGHTFULLY OUT A WINDOW" SONG:

5. THE "SUPER HOT SEX" SONG:

6. THE "I HATE EVERYTHING" SONG:

7. THE SONG THAT NEVER FAILS TO CHEER ME UP:

8. THE "GETTING READY TO GO TO A POTENTIALLY COOL PARTY" SONG:

9. THE "GETTING READY TO GO TO A POTENTIALLY LAME PARTY" SONG:

10. THE "PAINFUL BREAK-UP" SONG:

11. THE "PSYCH YOURSELF UP" SONG:

12. THE SONG THAT MAKES ME MISS YOU:

13. THE SONG THAT FEELS LIKE IT WAS WRITTEN ABOUT ME:

DRAW ALBUM ART :

WHAT'S
POPPIN'?

Pet Peeves

THINGS
I
THOUGHT
I'D
HAVE
FIGURED
OUT
BY
NOW

What's up, buttercup?

On the following page, write a letter to someone who is very meaningful to you at the moment.

THE SAD TRUTH is that relationships, no matter the nature, usually don't last forever. Someone you were super close to a year ago may feel like a stranger now.

I'm sure you know all of this already, but you may not know that you are holding onto some intense unsaid shit.

GIVE THE LETTER TO THEM OR KEEP IT FOR YOURSELF. EITHER WAY, LET THOSE EMOTIONS FLOWWW!

FUCK!
FUCK!
Fuck!
Fuck! I'm _____

A MOOD GRAPH
FOR THE MONTH OF _____

Track your emotions to get a better sense of them. Now when someone asks how you're doing, you can give them a more annoyingly accurate response!

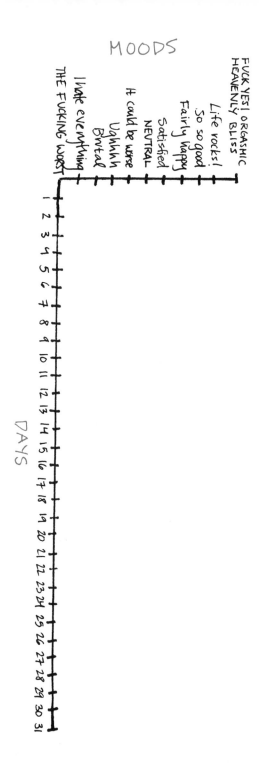

MOODS

FUCK YES! ORGASMIC
HEAVENLY BLISS
Life rocks!
So so good
Fairly happy
Satisfied
NEUTRAL
It could be worse
Ughhhh
Brutal
I hate everything
THE FUCKING WORST

1 2 3 4 5 6 7 8 9 10 11 12 13 14 15 16 17 18 19 20 21 22 23 24 25 26 27 28 29 30 31

DAYS

DISH TO ME

Overheard gems

[A log for all the incredible things you hear
while "accidentally" eavesdropping in public]

DATE: _____ TIME: _____ WHERE: _____
WHO: _____
WHAT WAS SAID: _____
_____
_____

DATE: _____ TIME: _____ WHERE: _____
WHO: _____
WHAT WAS SAID: _____
_____
_____

DATE: _____ TIME: _____ WHERE: _____
WHO: _____
WHAT WAS SAID: _____
_____
_____

DATE: _____ TIME: _____ WHERE: _____

WHO: _____

WHAT WAS SAID: _____

_____

_____

DATE: _____ TIME: _____ WHERE: _____

WHO: _____

WHAT WAS SAID: _____

_____

_____

DATE: _____ TIME: _____ WHERE: _____

WHO: _____

WHAT WAS SAID: _____

_____

_____

DATE: _____ TIME: _____ WHERE: _____

WHO: _____

WHAT WAS SAID: _____

_____

_____

What's cookin', good lookin'?

hand drawn instagrams

MY BREAKFAST

STREET SIGN THAT'S
BEEN TAMPERED WITH

NATURE
(e.g. sunset or
cool view)

MY FRIENDS

SCREEN SHOT OF
FUNNY TEXT CONVO

CUTE ANIMAL
DOING SOMETHING CUTE

MY FEET

CUTE BABY
DOING SOMETHING CUTE

WEIRD THING ON THE
SIDEWALK

Draw a safe
Place to go
think

fuckfuckfuckfuck

 What are you <u>nervously</u> <u>anticipating</u>?

 **BEST** POSSIBLE OUTCOME:

 **WORST** POSSIBLE OUTCOME:

UPDATE!

tell me what ended up happening. i'm on the edge of my seat! was it better or worse than you expected?

a Compare & Contrast Evaluation

MY INTERNET PERSONA

VS.

MY REAL IDENTITY

VENT TO ME

BFF TRADING CARDS

FRONT

BACK

FRONT

BACK

Tell me something good. ~~Tell me that you love me~~
or whatever

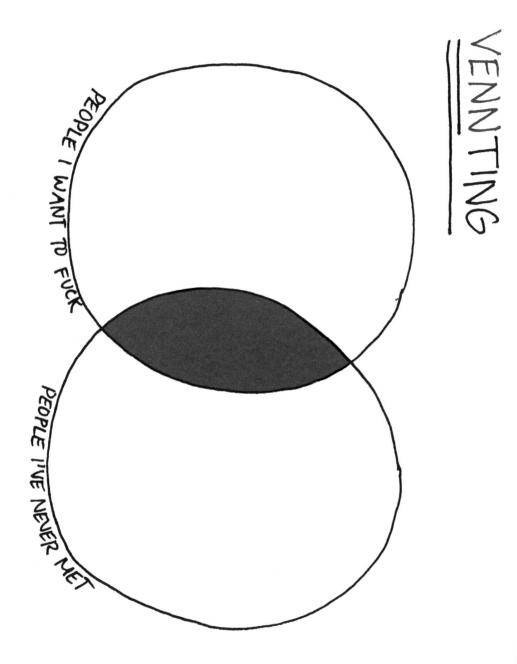

VENNTING

PEOPLE I WANT TO FUCK

PEOPLE I'VE NEVER MET

A PLACE FOR DRUNK RAMBLINGS

PLEASE DRINK! WRITE RESPONSIBLY

WRITE OUT A TYPICAL CONVERSATION WITH YOUR PARENTS

Do you only discuss certain topics? Do you fall into a pattern? Do you transform into some version of yourself that only they see?

current employment:

what's it like?

how's your relationship with your boss/
colleagues/customers?

where do you wanna go from here?

DISH TO ME

A freeform writing piece on how I treat others

be honest

What I'm Grateful For:

(DON'T SKIP THIS ONE, YOU JADED CYNIC!)

What's up, buttercup?

My Typical Daily Routine

DO YOU EVEN HAVE ONE? I'M STILL FIGURING MINE OUT. BUT I'M CLOSE! KIND OF... BUT REALLY, WHAT IS A STANDARD DAY LIKE FOR YOU?

The Daily Routine  I WISH I HAD

YOUR IDEAL DAY, FREE FROM YOUR REALITY

IS   IT   POSSIBLE?

SNAP  CHAT

WRITE WHATEVER THE FUCK YOU WANT!
AND THEN RIP THIS PAGE OUT AND THROW
IT AWAY/BURN IT/TEAR IT INTO A
THOUSAND PIECES!

FUCK!
FUCK!
Fuck!
Fuck! I'm _____

there's a time and a place for self-deprecation. for me, it's all the time and everywhere. but it's also important to figure out how to be nice to yourself. take this opportunity to remind yourself of your STRENGTHS

DRAW YOUR FAMILY PORTRAIT → whatever that means to you

WHAT'S
POPPIN'?

THINGS I WISH I COULD SAY OUT LOUD, BUT I CAN'T

I want to...

I love...

I hate...

I don't know...

I've always...

I...

VENT TO ME

people watching

A SERIES OF DRAWINGS
AND WORDS
IMAGINE
THE LIVES
THEY ARE
LEADING

What's cookin', good lookin'?

INSPIRATION STATION

← yeah, it's a dumb rhyme, but WHATEVA!

What articles, movies, songs, TV shows, books, fuckin' blogs + real live human beings are inspiring you right now?

DISH TO ME

I'm feeling LIKE SHIT today

DATE:

REASON:

I'm feeling **AMAZING** today

DATE:

REASON:

yesyesyesyesyes yesnoyesnoyesnomaybeyesnomaybe

Crushes on Strangers
that I'll never see again

PLACE:
WHAT THEY LOOKED LIKE:

FIRST FANTASY THAT WENT THROUGH MY HEAD:

PLACE:
WHAT THEY LOOKED LIKE:

FIRST FANTASY THAT WENT THROUGH MY HEAD:

PLACE:
WHAT THEY LOOKED LIKE:

FIRST FANTASY THAT WENT THROUGH MY HEAD:

PEOPLE I COMPARE MYSELF TO

[even though I know I shouldn't]

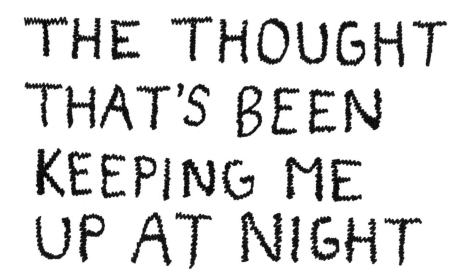

DISH TO ME

fictional characters I'd like to date
(if this leads to some erotic fan fiction, so be
it. you do you, boo.)

What's cookin', good lookin'?

MY ULTIMATE SEXUAL FANTASY

WHAT'S
POPPIN'?

TOP FIVE PRIORITIES

1.

2.

3.

4.

5.

Have these morphed in the last few years?
Is there something you wish was or wasn't on
this list?

Tell me something good. ~~Tell me that you love me~~
or whatever

self portrait

DRAW YOUR FUTURE SELF.

THE TEN YEAR PLAN

(SUBJECT TO CHANGE)

In one year, I want to...

In two years, I want to...

In three years, I want to...

In four years, I want to...

In five years, I want to...

In six years, I want to...

In seven years, I want to...

In eight years, I want to...

In nine years, I want to...

In ten years, I want to...

world predictions

Is it gonna be like 1984 Blade Runner Minority Report Are we gonna all have microchips in our brains? Are we gonna eat paper? I don't know! you tell me!!

DISH TO ME

Questions For My Future Self

FUCKING VISION BOARD NONSENSE

DRAW WHAT YOU WANT TO CONJURE IN YOUR LIFE

VENT TO ME

fuckfuckfuckfuck

predictions/desires

FOR YOUR FRIENDS

where do you hope to see them 5 or 10 years from now?

QUALITIES I'M LOOKING FOR IN MY IDEAL SIGNIFICANT OTHER:

Ok, ok. That's pretty good. But remember that no one is looking. Be as selfish and unrealistic as you want. Dig into that real shit that you'd never admit out loud. I won't tell!

goal checklist

FUCK!
FUCK!
Fuck!
Fuck! I'm _____